The King's Star

Written by RK Nelson and Adrianna Sharp
Illustrated by Bryce Westervelt

The King's Star © Copyright 2016 by RK Nelson and Adrianna Sharp

Divine Physiology Ministries Publisher
Nashville, Tennessee

All rights reserved

ISBN 978-0-9983379-0-6

Dewey Decimal Classification: 234
Subject Heading: JESUS CHRIST – NATIVITY\GOSPEL\SALVATION

Unless otherwise stated all Scripture quotations are from the Holy Bible, New Living Translation, Tyndale House, Carol Stream, IL, March, 2006.

Printed by IngramSpark
Nashville, Tennessee

To my wonderful family, especially my children and grandchildren! Your every day, ordinary conversation puts a smile on my face, inspires timeless truths in our sheer existence, the purpose and meaning of life and most of all God's love to us, our love in return to Him and to each other. I am greatly blessed for having each of you in my life!

Children are a gift from the LORD;
they are a reward from him.
Psalm 127:3 (Holy Bible New Living Translation)

Leaving church one Christmas Eve, a little girl did upward gaze. Look she said and pointed up, high up in the darkened haze.

Twinkle, twinkle in the night sky she saw,
the lights danced swiftly as they shined for all.
One star glowed so big and bright.
It was a star that seemed so full of light.

Is that the star that shown that night? Did that star appear over Baby Jesus, the Saviour's head?

Not that star said Papaw smiling, but long ago a star shone bright. Brighter than those stars you see tonight.

Seen by angels, shepherds, and earthly kings.
It stood above a manger that first Christmas evening.

It told us of the promised one. A saviour to the world he came. Confirmed by prophets of Old and preachers from the New. In the city of David, in Bethlehem a Christ Child, the Lord, was born anew.

Lay in a manger at the tower of the flock.
Wrapped in swaddling clothes to keep him
warm and bound. His mother the Virgin Mary
was certainly proud, as shepherds glimpsed
his face as baby cooed aloud.

She kissed his sweet fingers and his wriggly toes. She watched as the starlight beamed upon his little nose. A special star it was in a way. A special star it was for that very special baby birthday.

Starlight crowned a newborn King. Angels worshiped him and praises to glory they did sing. Bright light in the night, high up, way up, in the darkened sky.

In a robe of flesh sweet baby Jesus came.
He was the son of God,
the newborn Jewish King.

I am glad baby Jesus came for me, she said.
I am happy that he came and lay in that
manger bed. He loves me as you say Papaw,
which means I am special as can be.

Because a King came from heaven far away, on Christmas Day to earth he came to be. I now know Baby Jesus loved me then, and the star in heaven reminds me of his true story again and again.

www.ingramcontent.com/pod-product-compliance
Lightning Source LLC
Chambersburg PA
CBHW061937290426
44113CB00025B/2940